Key Stage 2 Reading Comprehension

Author: Elizabeth Negus

© Copyright 2015 Elizabeth Negus

All rights reserved

This book shall not, by way of trade or otherwise, be lent, resold, hired out, or otherwise circulated without the prior consent of the copyright holder and the publisher in any form of binding or cover other than that in which it is published and without a similar condition including this condition being imposed on the subsequent purchaser. The use of its contents in any other media is also subject to the same conditions.

First Publication 2015

ISBN 978-1-910176-87-0

Second Publication 2017

ISBN 978-0-9956796-1-0

2017
Published by

Cerint Media
Essex
United Kingdom
www.cerintmedia.com

Contents

Reading Comprehension

Super Teacher	1
The Rainbow	6
Come Fly With Me	8
Roald Dahl	12
The Dead Sea	17
The Picture of Dorian Gray	20
The Sea Raiders	26
Hard Times	34
Answers	42
Glossary	46

Introduction

Intellect is a key text book written to stretch and develop pupils reading and writing skills. The primary aim is always 'to make learning fun' whilst developing the pupil to a high competence level in literacy. This unique quality of fun learning and developing a mastermind for literacy is what makes Intellect outstanding.

Learning Strategies

Improve language skills in a structured context: grammar and vocabulary exercises teach students to avoid common mistakes. Intellect provides clear explanations and extensive practice of the grammar needed for Common Entrance and SATs exams.

Skills Practice

Immerse students in a wide range of topics to develop reading, writing, thinking, creative and imaginative skills.

Exam Practice

Familiarise students with the Common Entrance and SATs tests through authentic tasks: A variety of challenging, lively topics provide thorough training in exam skills and high level language development.

Answers

An answers appendix gives suggested answers for tasks where appropriate. Answer space for all questions is given in the workbook, the size of the space indicating the expected length of the response. A glossary of useful terms is also included for pupils development.

If you get some questions wrong, check your answers against the ones given on the answer sheet. Use your dictionary and / or work closely with your helper to learn and remember why the answer given is correct. When checking your comprehension question, the key is to re-read carefully both the passage and the question and carefully think it through.

Reading Comprehension

The Super Teacher!

Henry Trimble was a nine year old boy who loved nature, people and things. He had a passion for many types of hobbies and activities. Indeed, he loved going out with his friends to do fun things such as playing football, telling jokes and teasing his friends. Henry was always regarded as being cheerful, helpful, caring, diligent but above all, peculiar. He seemed to have had the best qualities amongst his friends, and at school his teachers admired him because he was an outstanding pupil with commendable qualities. However, there was one snag with Henry; although he had several hobbies and interests, he never really perfected any of them!

One night, Henry sat up in his bed, in the tranquillity of the room and thought, "Hmm, in two days time, December 21st will be my birthday. I will ask mum and dad to buy me an electric guitar". Henry delighted himself in this thought because he always had a love for musical instruments like the violin, drums and flute.

This time he thought that if he had a guitar he could play beautiful songs for his special friend, Hannah. One of Henry's favourite songs was David Ingles, "In Him I Live and Have My Being". He knew all the words and would sing so heartily that everyone around would sing-a-long! He knew all the other song tracks of David Ingles; it sure inspired and motivated him to teach with a special joy in his heart.

On his birthday, Henry was pleasantly surprised to find that his parents had actually bought him a very smart electric guitar. He took his guitar to school every Thursday and practiced strumming and reading musical notes.

Henry's music teacher was a short, plump, middle-aged lady named Mrs Bedford. After many weeks of having lessons, Henry was now sure that music was his main interest. He had a natural flair for music and he noticed that whenever he sang and played, it brought love, joy and peace to him. His friends, family and even strangers were always very happy when Henry played.

"GREAT! At last, I now know what my true purpose in life is! I am going to teach music and change the world". His voice rang though out the streets. He jumped up and down on his bed, shouting, "If music be the food of love play on". Fifteen years later, Henry grew to be a fine young man who was gifted and talented in music. He graduated as a school teacher and taught Music and Physics. The music brought life and love to his pupils. Soon he was referred to as, "Henry the Super Teacher"!

His pupils marvelled at learning about Waves, Energy, Gravity, Light and Heat! "How did all of it come together," they asked? "Who holds the great, big world together"? They had so many searching questions that Super Teacher Henry, thought... "Perhaps there are millions of people who do not understand the world; I am going to teach the world. Hey everyone, have you ever wondered about the sun, moon and stars? Do you want to explore the universe? Well, now you can, you can, you can".

He bought a gigantic house and above the doorpost was a wooden plaque that had the word, "Peculiar". Hundreds of men, women and children came and joined Super Teacher Henry singing and playing; they learnt about the universe. Soon, word spread all over England!

Thousands of people were taught by Super Teacher Henry. He always had a lovely smile on his face when he sang and taught. The little boys and girls would say, "Mum, when I grow up I want to be a super teacher like Henry Trimble". Soon, Super Teacher Henry's teaching was reaching people all over the UK and many learnt about the joy of good music and through Physics, they understood the wonderful world in which they lived. Henry had changed the world by filling it with music of David Ingles! His pupils were so inspired that they became super teachers of Music and Physics just like Henry Trimble!

The Super Teacher - Questions

Circle one answer for each question.

1 According to the story, how old was Henry?

    a. 15   b. 9   c. 12   d. 8

2 Why was Henry regarded as a star pupil?

    a.   He loved football and guitars
    b.   He loved telling jokes and teasing his friends
    c.   He had several hobbies and interests
    d.   He was cheerful, helpful, caring, diligent, loving and peculiar

3 When is Henry's birthday?

    a. October 22nd   b. December 21 st
    c. June 21st   d. March 21 st

4 What three musical instructions did Henry had a love for?

    a.   Flute, guitar, drums   b.   Violin, guitar, oboe
    c.   Harp, flute, piano   d.   Violin, drums, flute

5 What was Henry's true purpose in life?

    a.   To teach music and change the world
    b.   To teach football and make people happy
    c.   To teach friends how to tell jokes
    d.   To teach about hobbies and interests

Circle one answer for each question.

6 Henry Trimble was called "Henry the Super Teacher"
   a. True   b. False

7 What two subjects did Henry teach?
   a. Music and Art   b. Physics and Football
   c. English and Maths   d. Music and Physics

8 Henry was described as gifted and talented.
   a. True   b. False

9 Which word is closest in meaning to the italicised word in the following sentence from paragraph three: "He had a natural flair for music and he noticed that whenever he sang and played it brought love, joy and peace to him. His friends, family and even strangers were always very happy when Henry played."
   a. Talent   b. Love   c. Pride   d. Desire

10 Did Henry's teaching change the lives of hundreds of people in the UK?
   a. True
   b. False

The Rainbow

The rainbow is an arch of seven beautiful, bright colours. It is possible to see a rainbow in the sky after the sun and rain meet at the right angle. Sometimes it is hard to see all the seven colours, but on some occasions you might be able to see a complete rainbow with its brilliant colours of red, green, yellow, orange, blue, indigo and violet.

The poet William Wordsworth wrote in one of his poems, "My heart leaps up when I behold a rainbow in the sky". He was referring to the pleasure and joy most of us feel when we lookup in the sky and see a rainbow.

Rainbows can be seen not just in rain but also mist, spray, fog, and dew. In fact, whenever there are water droplets in the air and light shining from behind at the right angle, you will see a rainbow. It is very interesting to note that when the sun appears lower in the sky, the rainbow will be higher in the sky. When the sun appears higher in the sky, the rainbow will be lower in the sky. When we are on the ground, we see an arch or semi-circle but people in aeroplanes get to see a full and complete rainbow.

When we wake up every morning and look out of our windows, we normally see the sun in the east; therefore, if you are interested in seeing a rainbow, you must face toward the west where it is raining. This is simply because rain showers weather often comes from the west. The morning rainbow warns us of rainfall. In the late afternoon or early evenings the sun is in the western sky; after a heavy rainfall or thunderstorm, it usually is moving toward the east, where you will see a rainbow.

You will notice that because rain showers happen more regularly in the late afternoon than in the early morning, you are more likely to see a rainbow in the afternoon than in the morning and this is one of the main reasons that we link the appearance of a rainbow with the start of the weather getting better and brighter!

The Rainbow - Questions

1 How many colours are there in the rainbow? _____

2 Name the colours of the rainbow? _____

_____

3 What is the name of the poet who felt joy and pleasure when he saw the rainbow in the sky? _____

4 What is the shape of the rainbow? _____

5 When is the best time of day to see a rainbow? _____

6 In The space provided, describe your first impression of a rainbow.

_____

_____

Come Fly with me

It is 7.30 on Wednesday morning and Gatwick airport is closed because of the heavy snowfall. The snow had formed a thick white blanket on the surrounding roads and on the tarmac. This made it impossible for planes to land safely; many of the passengers, especially the children, were loitering in the lobby to avoid getting bored. The parents looked anxious and spent hours checking the airport TV screens to see when the runways would be cleared. There were businessmen who had appointments to keep and were disappointed when the Air Traffic Control announced that incoming flights were diverted to Stansted Airport.

Mr. George W Thompson had worked as an airport manager for twenty-five years and his main role was making sure that passengers are always taken very good care of. He is used to comforting inexperienced flyers, finding lost property and even returning little children who have strayed away from their parents watchful eyes! He is attentive, caring and kind but above all, he has a warm and funny personality. In the worse situation, Mr. Thompson knows how to calm the passengers and solve their problems so that everyone is happy and content.

Last Christmas David and Michael, aged 9 and 10, were travelling for the first time without their parents. They were booked on the Boeing 747, one of Britain's top aeroplanes. David and Michael were also booked in the first class cabin so that they would get the best service. The first class cabin also offers very comfortable seats for relaxing in and sleeping.

At the airport, Mr. Thompson guided David and Michael through check-in and security. They checked their documents and weighed their bags.

Suddenly, the clock struck 11 which meant that the boys had one hour left before their flight. Realising this, Mr. George Thompson decided to take them to the VIP lounge for drinks and cakes. Excitedly, the boys raced down the aisle with Mr. Thompson trying desperately not to crash into oncoming passengers. The boys felt safe and happy in Mr. Thompson's company because he was friendly and approachable. They were giggling all the way to the lounge; Mr. Thompson was also joyfully enjoying taking care of the boys; a sense of pride engulfed him as passengers watched David and Michael swinging on his arms and tugging at his sleeves. It was clear that he loved his job as airport manager!

Come fly with me - Questions

1 What is the name of the airport that was closed?

_____

2 Why was the airport closed?

_____

3 What is the name of the airport manager?

_____

4 How long has he been employed at the airport?

_____

Come fly with me - Questions

5 What are the names of the children in his care?
_____

6 How is Mr. Thompson described in the passage?
_____

7 What makes you think Mr. Thompson loves his job?
_____

Come fly with me - Sentence

Write a sentence containing each word below to show you understand its meaning.

a tarmac
_____

b loitering
_____

Come fly with me - Sentence

c diverted
_____

d strayed
_____

e solve
_____

f content
_____

Roald Dahl

Adapted from Roald Dahl: A Biography by Jeremy Treglown

Read the following brief biography of a famous children's writer.

Roald Dahl was born on 13th September 1916 in Llandaff, South Wales; his parents were born in Norway. Roald's father died while he was still a child. Dahl was good at cricket and swimming, but did not perform very well in class. Dahl had many hobbies but one of his main hobbies was reading, and some of his favourite novelists were the adventure writers, Rudyard Kipling and H. Rider Haggard. He was also interested in greyhound dogs, paintings and antiques.

Dahl wrote many interesting novels; he wrote Boy, Danny Champion of the World, The Landlady, and many more. Much of his writings came from the personal experiences he had at different boarding schools. He attended Llandaff Cathedral School for just two years. Then from the ages of nine to thirteen he attended St. Peter's Preparatory School in Weston-SuperMare, England. He did not enjoy the school because many of the teachers were cruel and often punished the students by caning them.

When Dahl was thirteen his family moved to Kent in England, and he was sent to Repton Public School. Repton was much harsher than his old school. The headmaster enjoyed beating children and the older students used the younger ones as servants. However, there was one good thing about the school. Every few months the chocolate company, Cadburys, sent boxes of chocolates to Repton for the students to test. This happy memory gave Dahl the idea for his most famous novel, Charlie and the Chocolate Factory.

In 1939 World War II started. Dahl joined the RAF (Royal Air Force) and learned to fly warplanes. Unfortunately, on his first flight, his plane ran out of fuel and crashed in the Libyan desert. He fractured his skull but managed to crawl out of the burning plane.

It was during World War II (1939 to 1945) that Dahl became a writer. He wrote a short story about his adventures as a fighter pilot for the Royal Air Force. The story was so very interesting that the Saturday Evening Post bought it. This was the start of Dahl's long career as a writer. He wrote novels for adults and while living in England, he took time out to write children's stories. His well-known children's stories that were made into films were James and the Giant Peach and Charlie and the Chocolate Factory. He won many awards including the Children's Book Award.

When Dahl left school he decided that he wanted to travel. He got a job with the Shell Oil Company and two years later was sent to East Africa. In his autobiography, Going Solo, he writes about some of the exciting adventures there, including the time a black mamba entered his friend's house and a snake catcher had to be called in.

Roald Dahl died on 23rd November 1990 in Oxford, England.

Roald Dahl- Questions

1 What do you think the word 'biography' means?

_____

_____

2 When and where was Roald Dahl born?

_____

_____

3 What was Dahl's main hobby?

_____

4 What were Dahl's main interests?

_____

_____

Roald Dahl- Questions

5 List four books that Dahl wrote.

a. _____

b. _____

c. _____

d. _____

6 List the names of three schools that Dahl went to as a child.

a. _____

b. _____

c. _____

7 Why did Dahl hate the schools he attended?

_____

_____

Roald Dahl- Questions

8 Which two novels did Dahl write and were adapted into films?

a. _____

b. _____

9 When did Dahl become a writer?

_____

10 In what year did Dahl die?

_____

The Dead Sea

Did you know that the Dead Sea is the lowest lake on Earth? The Dead Sea lies in a desert and rainfall is very irregular. The River Jordan, one of the largest rivers in the world, flows into the Dead Sea mainly in winter and spring. When you look at the Dead Sea, you will notice that it is very calm and deep blue in colour.

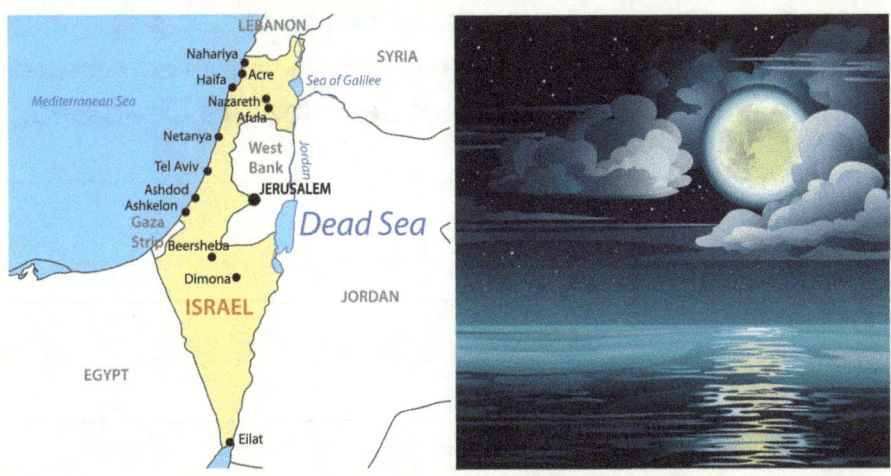

The water is extremely salty, and because of this, there is hardly any fish living in it. For this reason, it is very difficult for marine life to survive except for a few single celled organisms that have got used to the hostile water. Sometimes fish accidentally swim into the waters from one of the several freshwater streams that feed the Sea and are killed instantly. Their dead bodies are quickly covered with a layer of salt crystals and then tossed onto shore by the wind and waves. Human beings who bathe in the water are not affected. They remain healthy except that their skin gets dry and crusty after a salty swim.

The white crystals of salt covering the sea shore, is not ordinary table salt. The salts found in the Dead Sea are mineral salts, just like you find in the oceans of the world, only that it is highly concentrated.

Scientists claim that around 35% of the water in the Dead Sea is salt! That means the Dead Sea is six times saltier than the ocean! The deeper you swim out into the Dead Sea the saltier it gets. Near the bottom of the Dead Sea the salt is so concentrated that the water gets hard and turns into salt crystals and settles on the sea floor.

The Dead Sea - Questions

1 What is the name of the lowest lake on Earth?

_____

2 Write three simple sentences that describe the Dead Sea.

a. _____

_____

b. _____

_____

c. _____

_____

3 What happens to the fish that accidentally swim into the Dead Sea?

_____

_____

_____

18

The Dead Sea - Questions

4 What happens to people who swim in the Dead Sea?

_____

_____

5 What percentage of the water is salt?

_____

_____

6 What happens to the water when it is concentrated with salt?

_____

_____

The Picture of Dorian Gray

This is an abridged extract from the novel The Picture of Dorian Gray by Oscar Wilde.

After about a quarter of an hour Hallward stopped painting, looked for a long time at Dorian Gray, and then for a long time at the picture, biting the end of one of his huge brushes and frowning. "It is quite finished," he cried at last, and stooping down he wrote his name in long vermilion letters on the left-hand corner of the canvas.

Lord Henry came over and examined the picture. It was certainly a wonderful work of art, and a wonderful likeness as well.

"My dear fellow, I congratulate you most warmly," he said. "It is the finest portrait of modern times. Mr. Gray, come over and look at yourself."

The lad started, as if awakened from some dream.

"Is it really finished?" he murmured, stepping down from the platform.

"Quite finished," said the painter. "And you have sat splendidly today. I am awfully obliged to you."

"That is entirely due to me," broke in Lord Henry. "Isn't it, Mr. Gray?"

Dorian made no answer, but passed listlessly in front of his picture and turned towards it. When he saw it he drew back, and his cheeks flushed for a moment with pleasure. A look of joy came into his eyes, as if he had recognised himself for the first time. He stood there motionless and in wonder, dimly conscious that Hallward was speaking to him, but not catching the meaning of his words. The sense of his own beauty came on him like a revelation. He had never felt it before. Basil Hallward's compliments had seemed to him to be merely the charming exaggeration of friendship. He had listened to them, laughed at them, forgotten them.

They had not influenced his nature. Then had come Lord Henry Wotton with his strange panegyric on youth, his terrible warning of its brevity. That had stirred him at the time, and now, as he stood gazing at the shadow of his own loveliness, the full reality of the description flashed across him. Yes, there would be a day when his face would be wrinkled and wizen, his eyes dim and colourless, the grace of his figure broken and deformed. The scarlet would pass away from his lips and the gold steal from his hair. The life that was to make his soul would mar his body. He would become dreadful, hideous, and
uncouth.

As he thought of it, a sharp pang of pain struck through him like a knife and made each delicate fibre of his nature quiver. His eyes deepened into amethyst, and across them came a mist of tears. He felt as if a hand of ice had been laid upon his heart.

    "Don't you like it?" cried Hallward at last, stung a little by the lad's silence, not understanding what it meant.
    "Of course he likes it," said Lord Henry. "Who wouldn't like it? It is one of the greatest things in modern art. I will give you anything you like to ask for it. I must have it."
    "It is not my property, Harry."
    "Whose property is it?"
    "Dorian's, of course," answered the painter.
    "He is a very lucky fellow."
    "How sad it is!" murmured Dorian Gray with his eyes still fixed upon his own portrait. "How sad it is! I shall grow old, and horrible, and dreadful. But this picture will remain always young. It will never be older than this particular day of June. . . . If it were only the other way! If it were I who was to be always young, and the picture that was to grow old!
For that--for that--I would give everything! Yes, there is nothing in the whole world I would not give!

The Picture of Dorian Gray - Questions

1 From the second paragraph, what does the phrase "work of art" mean?

_____

_____

2 How does Dorian react to his portrait?

_____

_____

3 What does Dorian say about himself?

_____

_____

The Picture of Dorian Gray - Questions

4 Wilde makes use of similes and metaphors in the passage to create vivid pictures in the reader's mind. Find two examples of similes and metaphors in the passage.

a. _____

b. _____

c. _____

d. _____

5 Why is Dorian desperate to stay young? Support your answer with a quote from the passage.

_____
_____
_____

The Picture of Dorian Gray - Questions

6 Read the paragraph starting with Dorian made no answer, ... to He would become dreadful, hideous, and uncouth.

What do you understand by the phrase "wrinkled and wizen"?

_____

_____

_____

_____

7 Find synonyms for the following words in the table

Ignoble				
Hideous				
Uncouth				

The Picture of Dorian Gray - Questions

8 Why do you think the novel is called "The Picture of Dorian Gray"?

_____

_____

The Sea Raiders

This is an extract from the short story The Sea Raiders by H G Wells

This Comprehension is mearnt to stretch and challenge readers. After reading make a good attempt at answering the questions.

Mr. Fison, torn by curiosity, began picking his way across the waveworn rocks, and finding the wet seaweed that covered them thickly rendered them extremely slippery, he stopped, removed his shoes and socks, and rolled his trousers above his knees. His object was, of course, merely to avoid stumbling into the rocky pools about him, and perhaps he was rather glad, as all men are, of an excuse to resume, even for a moment, the sensations of his boyhood. At any rate, it is to this, no doubt, that he owes his life.

He approached his mark with all the assurance which the absolute security of this country against all forms of animal life gives its inhabitants. The round bodies moved to and fro, but it was only when he surmounted the of boulders I have mentioned that he realised the horrible nature of the discovery. It came upon him with some suddenness.

The rounded bodies fell apart as he came into sight over the ridge, and displayed the pinkish object to be the partially devoured body of a human being, but whether of a man or woman he was unable to say.

And the rounded bodies were new and ghastly-looking creatures, in shape somewhat resembling an octopus, with huge and very long and flexible tentacles, coiled copiously on the ground. The skin had a glistening texture, unpleasant to see, like shiny leather.

The downward bend of the tentacle-surrounded mouth, the curious excrescence at the bend, the tentacles, and the large intelligent eyes, gave the creatures a grotesque suggestion of a face. They were the size of a fair-sized swine about the body, and the tentacles seemed to him to be many feet in length. There were, he thinks, seven or eight at least of the creatures. Twenty yards beyond them, amid the surf of the now returning tide, two others were emerging from the sea.

Their bodies lay flatly on the rocks, and their eyes regarded him with evil interest; but it does not appear that Mr. Fison was afraid, or that he realised that he was in any danger. Possibly his confidence is to be ascribed to the limpness of their attitudes. But he was horrified, of course, and intensely excited and indignant, at such revolting creatures preying upon human flesh. He thought they had chanced upon a drowned body. He shouted to them, with the idea of driving them off, and finding they did not budge, cast about him, picked up a big rounded lump of rock, and flung it at one.

And then, slowly uncoiling their tentacles, they all began moving towards him--creeping at first deliberately, and making a soft purring sound to each other.

The Sea Raiders - Questions

1 What did Mr Fison find on the rocky shoreline?

_____
_____
_____

2 In paragraph one, what does the phrase "picking his way" mean?

_____
_____
_____

3 List three things that Mr Fison did to avoid slipping on the rocks which were covered with wet seaweed?

a. _____

b. _____

c. _____

The Sea Raiders - Questions

4 **Art Work**

In the box provided, draw a picture of one of the pictures described in paragraph 3

5 Why was Mr Fison not afraid of the evil looking creatures?

_____
_____

6 Wells uses a simile in the extract. Write out the simile in the lines provided.

_____
_____
_____

The Sea Raiders - Questions

7 Write out four phrases that describe the creatures.

a. _____

b. _____

c. _____

d. _____

8 Find synonyms for the following words in the table

surmounted				
copiously				
confidence				

The Sea Raiders - Questions

indignant				
revolting				
flexible				

9 **Improve my Knowledge:** Learning about Britain in the nineteenth century.

Using books and web-sites, find out what life was like with the below listed words for people who lived during the reign of Queen Victoria.

a **Country Life**

_____
_____
_____

The Sea Raiders - Questions

b) Life in Towns

c) Life for the Rich

d) Life for the Poor

The Sea Raiders - Questions

e. Food and Drink

_____
_____
_____

f. Health and Medicine

_____
_____
_____

g. Women and Chidren

_____
_____
_____

Hard Times

This is an extract from the novel Hard Times by Charles Dickens

... Let us strike the key-note, Coketown, before pursuing our tune.

It was a town of red brick, or of brick that would have been red if the smoke and ashes had allowed it; but as matters stood, it was a town of unnatural red and black like the painted face of a savage. It was a town of machinery and tall chimneys, out of which interminable serpents of smoke trailed themselves for ever and ever, and never got uncoiled. It had a black canal in it, and a river that ran purple with ill-smelling dye, and vast piles of building full of windows where there was a rattling and a trembling all day long, and where the piston of the steam-engine worked monotonously up and down, like the head of an elephant in a state of melancholy madness. It contained several large streets all very like one another, and many small streets still more like one another, inhabited by people equally like one another, who all went in and out at the same hours, with the same sound upon the same pavements, to do the same work, and to whom every day was the same as yesterday and to-morrow, and every year the counterpart of the last and the next.

These attributes of Coketown were in the main inseparable from the work by which it was sustained; against them were to be set off, comforts of life which found their way all over the world, and elegancies of life which made, we will not ask how much of the fine lady, who could scarcely bear to hear the place mentioned. The rest of its features were voluntary, and they were these.

You saw nothing in Coketown but what was severely workful. If the members of a religious persuasion built a chapel there - as the members of eighteen religious persuasions had done - they made it a pious warehouse of red brick, with sometimes (but this is only in highly ornamental examples) a bell in a birdcage on the top of it.

The solitary exception was the New Church; a stuccoed edifice with a square steeple over the door, terminating in four short pinnacles like florid wooden legs. All the public inscriptions in the town were painted alike, in severe characters of black and white. The jail might have been the infirmary, the infirmary might have been the jail, the town-hall might have been either, or both, or anything else, for anything that appeared to the contrary in the graces of their construction. Fact, fact, fact, everywhere in the material aspect of the town; fact, fact, fact, everywhere in the immaterial. The M'Choakumchild school was all fact, and the school of design was all fact, and the relations between master and man were all fact, and everything was fact between the lying-in hospital and the cemetery, and what you couldn't state in figures, or show to be purchasable in the cheapest market and saleable in the dearest, was not, and never should be, world without end, Amen.

Hard Times - Questions

1 Why is Coketown written in capital letters?

_____
_____
_____

2 In paragraph two, select and write out the similes and metaphors under their appropriate in the table below.

Similes	Metaphors
a. _____	_____
b. _____	_____
c. _____	_____
d. _____	_____

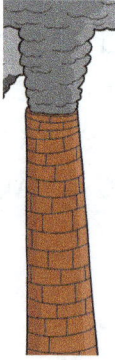

Hard Times - Questions

3 **Re-read paragraph two.** Explain clearly the image that is created about Coketown?

_____

_____

_____

_____

4 In paragraph four, what does the phrase 'religious persuasion' mean?

_____

_____

_____

5 In paragraph four, why does Dickens repeat the words 'fact, fact, fact'?

_____

_____

Hard Times - Questions

6 List three words or phrases that tell the readers that Hard Times was written in the Nineteenth century?

a. _____

b. _____

c. _____

7 List four main characteristics of Coketown.

a. _____

b. _____

c. _____

d. _____

Hard Times - Questions

8 **Re-read paragraph two.** Explain clearly what life was like for the people of Coketown?

_____
_____
_____
_____
_____

Improve my Knowledge: More questions about the novel Hard Times by Charles Dickens

9 Who was Charles Dickens?

_____
_____

10 What was London like during Charles Dickens time?

_____
_____
_____

Hard Times - Questions

11. Dickens wrote fifteen novels in total. List nine of these novels in the box below to show your literary knowledge.

12. Write four facts about the ragged school.

a. _____

b. _____

c. _____

d. _____

Hard Times - Questions

13 Write five facts about life in the nineteenth century during the reign of Queen Victoria.

a. _____

b. _____

c. _____

d. _____

e. _____

14 Have you been to the Charles Dickens Museum?

_____
_____
_____

Answers

Pages 4-5 - The Super Teacher!

1. b) 9
2. d) He was cheerful, helpful, caring, diligent, loving and peculiar
3. b) December 21st
4. d) Violin, drums, flute
5. a) To teach music and change the world
6. a) True
7. d) Music and Physics
8. a) True
9. a) Talent
10. a) True

Page 7 - The Rainbow

1. There are seven colours in the rainbow.
2. The colours of the rainbow are red, green, yellow, orange, blue, indigo and violet.
3. William Wordsworth
4. The rainbow is an arch or semicircle.
5. The best time of day to see a rainbow is in the afternoon.

Pages 9-11 - Come Fly with Me

1. Gatwick airport
2. Gatwick airport was closed because of the heavy snowfall.
3. The name of the airport manager is Mr. George W Thompson.
4. He has worked as an airport manager for twenty-five years.
5. The names of the children in his care are David and Michael.
6. Mr. Thompson is described as being attentive, caring and kind but above all, he has a warm and funny personality.
7. I think Mr. Thompson loves his job because he was happy guiding David and Michael through the airport and on to their flight. He did not mind the boys swinging on his arms and he too was giggling with the boys.

Sentences containing the words below Answers may vary.

a. tarmac - The planes landed safely on the tarmac.
b. loitering- Jack was put on detention for loitering in the library.
c. diverted- The traffic was diverted because of the accident on the A 12.
d. strayed- Mrs. Binkey fed the strayed cat for six years.
e. solve- It is important to solve problems at all times.
f. content- I am content with all my English grades; I feel very confident at the moment.

Pages 14-16 - Roald Dahl

1. The story of a person's life, written by someone else.
2. Roald Dahl was born on 13th September 1916 in Llandaff, South Wales.
3. One of his main hobbies was reading.
4. He was also interested in greyhound dogs, paintings and antiques.
5. Boy, Danny Champion of the World, The Landlady, Charlie and the Chocolate Factory.
6. Llandaff Cathedral School, St Peter's Preparatory School, Repton Public School.

Answers

7. He did not enjoy the school because many of the teachers were cruel and often punished the students by caning them.

8. Charlie and the Chocolate Factory, James and the Giant Peach.

9. It was during World War II (1939 to 1945) that Dahl became a writer.

10. Roald Dahl died on 23rd 1990 in Oxford, England.

Page 18-19 - The Dead Sea

1. The Dead Sea

2. a. The Dead Sea is very calm.
b. The Dead Sea is deep blue in colour.
c. The water is extremely salty.

3. The fish are killed instantly.

4. They remain healthy except that their skin gets dry and crusty after a salty swim.

5. Scientists claim that around 35% of the water in the Dead Sea is salt!

6. The water gets hard and turns in to salt crystals and settles on the sea bed.

Pages 22-25 - The Picture of Dorian Gray by Oscar Wilde

1. A painting or picture with strong imaginative and creative appeal; a picture or painting that is very attractive, a picture or painting with skilful detail.

2. (Answers will vary)-he feels a sense of despair, sadness, depression, feeling low and lifeless, miserable, helpless because he cannot stay young forever and will one day grow old

3. "I shall grow old, and horrid and dreadful, but the picture will stay young".

4.
Similes
a. a shape pang of pain struck like a knife
b. his own beauty came on him like a revelation

Metaphors
c. a mist of tears
d. hand of ice

5. Answers will vary, either a or b is ok.
a. afraid of growing old – "his face will be wrinkled and wizen, his eyes dim and colourless, the grace of his figure broken and deformed"
b. he wants to keep the joy of his loveliness and beauty; being old makes him sad; it would "mar his body" and he would become " ignoble, hideous, and uncouth"

6. to become dry, shrunken because of old age; to have a crinkled ugly face caused by old age

7. synonyms for the following words in red

Ignoble	unworthy	shameful	shabby	degraded
Hideous	ugly	repulsive	disgusting	horrific
Uncouth	rough	crude	gross	ill-mannered

Answers

8. Answers will vary.
a) it focuses on the painting of Dorian Gray
b) we learn a great deal about how Dorian is affected by the painting
c) the painting is the subject matter in the passage

Pages 28-33 - The Sea Raiders by H G Wells

1. Ghastly looking creatures, resembling an octopus, with huge and very long and flexible tentacles; half eaten human bodies.

2. (Answers will vary)-To make his way through, to move along his route on foot through the rocky area. To work slowly and carefully through a dangerous route.

3.
a) he stopped
b) he removed his shoes and socks
c) coiled his trousers above his knees

4. Developing Imaginative and Creative Skills (You should have drawn a picture of one of the creatures described in paragraph 3.)

5. He was a confident man; he was not aware that he was in danger; he was furious that these revolting creatures could prey on humans.

6. The skin had a glistening texture, unpleasant to see, like shiny leather.

7. Answers will vary.
a) they were the size of a fair-sized swine
b) they had flat bodies...evil eyes
c) creatures had the shape of an octopus
d) creatures had very long and flexible tentacles

8. synonyms for the following words in red

surmounted	exceeded	out done	rose above	over power
copiously	plentifully	abundantly	extensively	fully
confidence	trust	faith	surety	hope
indignant	annoyed	furious	resentful	upset
revolting	shocking	foul	horrible	appalling
flexible	adjustable	manageable	yielding	adaptable

Pages 36-41 - Hard Times by Charles Dickens

1. Answers may vary along these lines:
a) Capitals provide visibility
b) Shouts at the reader
c) Emphasises importance
d) Draws reader's attention
e) Allows reader to focus on the word and its relevance to the text

2. Paragraph two similes and metaphors

Similes
a. black like the painted face of a savage
b. machine worked monotonously up and down like the head of an elephant
c. everyday was the same as yesterday and tomorrow

Metaphors
c. interminable serpents of smoke
d. in a state of melancholy madness

Answers

3. Answers will vary for image that is created about Coketown. Any of the below is accepted.

a) The colours red and black are used to describe the city. Red is the color of brick as well as blood, black is the colour of ashes and smoke but it also reminds to hell and death. The "unnatural" colours are compared with the savage's face to stress the horrifying atmosphere and landscape of the city. The machinery, chimneys, piston, steam-engine creates an image of a very dirty and unhygienic place, terribly hard work and lots of noise. The metaphors and similes are linked to the semantic field of animals. The serpent is often associated with sin and the devil.

b) Coketown is a boring place to live and work because every day is the same.

c) The ill-smelling dye and the rattling and trembling of windows paints an image of disused warehouses, jails, and polluted environments.

d) The red brick stained with the black caused by the coal burning steam engines in the factories is likened to the painted face of a savage; this image is negative, describing something frightening and ghastly.

4. To have a particular belief or idea about a religious group, religion.

5. It emphasises Dickens message and keeps it in the reader's mind. The reader will want to keep on reading.

6. three phrases that tell the readers Hard Times was written in the nineteenth century?

a) taint of fancy

b) pursuing our tune

c) town of machinery

7. four main characteristics of Coketown: Answers will vary.

a) it was a town of red brick

b) it was a town of machinery and tall chimneys

c) it contained several large streets which all looked the same

d) Coketown was a place of constant hard work

8. what life was like for the people of Coketown?
Answers will vary.

Dickens's Coketown is shown as dirty, polluted, unpleasant, and a monotonous place to live in. Coketown is a place of suffering and exploitation. The characters work all day with no forms of enjoyment.

Glossary of Terms

This glossary presents brief explanations of terms often used in English language.

Adjective - The part of speech modifying the noun or pronoun: a red dress.
Adverb - The part of speech modifying a verb, an adjective or another adverb: quickly moving.
Colon - The colon introduces a list of things: rice, milk, break, cake, sugar, oil.
Comma - The comma separates items in a sentence: I like apples, plums, mangoes and grapes. The comma also separates phrases and some clauses.
Comprehension - The ability to understand something.
Exclamation mark - The exclamation mark shows feeling: Help!
Question mark - A punctuation symbol "?" written at the end of a sentence to indicate a direct question. How old are you?
Full stop/Period - A punctuation mark indicating the end of a sentence. The room is crowded.
Grammar - The study of sentence structure, especially with the use of correct sentences and correct vocabulary. I spoke to my teacher, Mr. Bright.
Metaphor - A figure of speech in which one thing is described in terms of another. Christine is a ray of sunshine.
Noun - A noun is the name given to a person, place or thing: ribbon, train, grass, flowers and shoe.
Parts of speech - The eight common parts of speech are the verb, noun, adjective, adverb, pronoun, preposition, conjunction, and interjection.
Prefix - A prefix is placed at the beginning of a word to change its meaning. Pre means "before." Prefixes may also indicate a location, number, or time. Root: central part of a word. dis-like, re-move, un-kind.
Preposition - A word which tells you where one thing is in relation to another. The mouse is under the table.

Glossary of Terms

Pronoun - The pronoun takes the place of a noun. Perry is playing badminton and he is winning.

Semicolon - The semicolon joins two closely related clauses in a sentence.

Sentence - A set of words which form a grammatically complete statement, usually containing a subject, verb, and object. The flowers are on the table.

Simile - A figure of speech in which one thing is directly likened to another by using the word as or like. Your face glows like the morning sun.

Suffix - The ending part of a word that changes the meaning of the word. Thank-ful, harm-less, wash-able.

Vocabulary - The particular selection or types of words chosen in speech or writing.